A Catholic Bishop

Let the Oppressed Go Free: Breaking the Bonds of Addiction

Cardinal Justin Rigali

BASILICA ™

P R E S S

Published by
Basilica Press
PO Box 610465
Dallas, TX 75261

Editor: Gerry Korson
Cover Design: Giuliana Gerber/ACI Prensa
Layout: Cheryl Vaca

Printed in the United States of America
ISBN 1-930314-14-0

Basilica Press is part of the
Joseph and Marie Daou Foundation.

TABLE OF CONTENTS

INTRODUCTION

The Church speaks on many issues of our time. Has the Church spoken a great deal on addiction?

The Church's mission, as entrusted to her by Jesus Christ and carried out under the impulse of the Holy Spirit, is a call to preach the Good News of the love of God the Father through the forgiveness of sins and the healing of those who are afflicted. The love of the Father is fully revealed in Jesus, in particular in his Passion, Death, and Resurrection. The pastoral activity of the Church, therefore, is directed in an immediate manner to the suffering and the afflicted.

The contemporary culture so often casts persons to the sidelines, and in their pain they sometimes seek out ways of coping that do further harm to their human dignity. Pastoral experience tells us that persons of all backgrounds and ages can be affected by addiction. The Church always calls us to appreciate and renew our dedication to the inviolable dignity of the human person. This is especially true in the area of addiction.

In the Old Testament, God announced his closeness to those who are suffering: "Is this not the fast which I choose:

To loosen the bonds of wickedness, to undo the bands of the yoke, and to let the oppressed go free and break every yoke?" (Is 58:6). The Church models her response on that of Jesus in the Gospel. Jesus directed his mission in a particular way to those afflicted and suffering. We read in the Gospel of St. Matthew: "[P]eople brought to him all who were ill with various diseases, those suffering severe pain ... and he healed them" (Mt 4:24 cf. 8:16; 9:1ff; 9:22). St. Mark tells us: "Jesus healed many who had various diseases" (Mk 1:32; cf. 1:42; 5:29; 7:35; 8:25; 9:27). St. Luke also recounts the healings that Jesus performed (Lk 4:40; 5:17; 7:10; 8:48; 9:42). St. John presents Jesus as the Good Shepherd (Jn 10:11) who seeks out the lost and heals the sick.

The Church has addressed addiction and psychological dependency in many ways. It has done this by calling for care for those who are addicted or dependent, by offering continued guidance for those in recovery, and by issuing a call for strategies aimed at the prevention of addiction. In a particular way, the Church has called attention to the underlying causes of addiction. Our Holy Father, Pope Benedict XVI, refers to the abuse of drugs in particular in his first encyclical letter *Deus Caritas Est* ("God is Love"): "The anti-culture of death, which finds expression for example in drug use, is thus countered by an unselfish love which shows itself to be a culture of life by the very willingness to 'lose itself' (cf. Lk 17:33 *et passim*) for others" (*DCE* 30).

Our late Holy Father, the Servant of God Pope John Paul II, often addressed the problem of addiction. He called upon youths to guard against the "scourge of alcohol and drugs" that obscures the real world and takes a heavy toll as it leads one to escape to a painful fantasy world. He emphasized that Christians cannot ignore these painful realities that lead to emptiness rather than happiness. He entrusted the ongoing pastoral concern for persons with addictions to the Pontifical Council for the Family. In 1991, the Pontifical Council promulgated the document "From Despair to Hope," which addressed issues of the family and drug addiction.

In speaking on addiction, Pope John Paul II referred to the words of Jesus from the Gospel of St. Luke: "If any man would come after me, let him deny himself and take up his cross daily and follow me" (Lk 9:23). Those who struggle with addiction are called to follow the path of discipleship in a particularly courageous way.

A Catholic response to addiction involves at least six elements:

1. There must be an understanding of the nature of addiction.

2. There must be an understanding of a robust Christian anthropology that understands the nature of the human person as a union of body and soul. As such, the human person tends toward the good but is wounded by sin. The person's struggle with the appetites is therefore augmented by need, pain, and fear. The person attempts to meet the intangible needs of the human heart through the appetites. This tendency mounts, and by the time it proves itself to be insufficient, it has completely overwhelmed the person, and he or she is caught in an addiction cycle. The Catholic teaching on grace and virtue can bring healing, recovery, and renewal to those who suffer the pain of addiction.

3. A Catholic response to addiction must include an initial appraisal of new dangers posed by the Internet as well as other new dangers stemming from a poor use of technology — for example, the abuse of mood-altering substances and other medical technology. It should also pay attention to the increasing phenomena of human isolation in an increasingly mechanized world, even as traditional social structures are threatened.

4. The healing and recovery from addiction and dependency must give primacy of place to the importance of grace and virtue received within the sacramental life of the Church.

5. We must consider the life of prayer in recovery.

6. Finally, we must examine faith-based governmental programs as well as various educational and behavioral programs, such as the various Twelve Step programs, that are compatible with recovery.

PART I:
THE NATURE OF ADDICTION

I. What is an addiction?

An addiction is a painful situation with very diverse factors. A person who has an addiction suffers with a physically dependent and detrimental relationship to a chemical or substance such as drugs or alcohol. The substance can range from common medications and prescription pharmaceuticals to illegal drugs. Related to addiction is psychological dependency, which may take the form of a harmful attachment to an event, activity, sensation, or relationship with another person. For example, gambling, acting out sexually, eating, video games, work, sports, achievement, approval, exercise, and shopping may become forms of psychological dependency.

In the midst of an addiction or dependency, a person experiences strong desires for the substance, event, or process, even when that substance, event, or process would be harmful in itself or would obscure some positive value in the person's life. (For the sake of simplicity, hereafter we will refer to both substance dependency and psychological dependency as "addiction.")

Addiction is characterized by desires that take the form of recurrent and insistent cravings and urges. These desires become so powerful that they consume a person's energy on at least a physiological, psychological, social, or spiritual level. The person seeks relief from the discomfort of these urges and cravings by carrying out a *cycle of addiction*, a sequence that commonly runs from indulgence to self-hating regret to resistance and back to indulgence. This sequence is an attempt to manage the cravings and quell the urges that impel the addict to reach some plateau of pleasure or momentary satisfaction. The repetition goes beyond the seeking of pleasure and becomes a series of self-defeating, shaming-and-blaming behaviors that compound stress rather than alleviate it. The person loses more and more control of his or her life as the time devoted to the addiction increasingly becomes a primary focus. The pattern is repeated so often and the person becomes accustomed to it on so many internal and external levels that they are virtually chained to the addictive behavior.

In all of this, personal freedom is greatly impeded and, in some cases, may even be taken away. I do not mean that they lose their autonomy, though in some cases they may come close to this. What I am referring to is the tremendous wounding of their freedom whereby they are enslaved to a substance, activity, or event. Pope John Paul II, in

Redemptor Hominis ("The Redeemer of Man"), his first encyclical letter, taught that freedom must be based on truth:

"Jesus Christ meets the man of every age, including our own, with the same words: 'You will know the truth, and the truth will make you free' (Jn 8:32). These words contain both a fundamental requirement and a warning: the requirement of an honest relationship with regard to truth as a condition for authentic freedom, and the warning to avoid every kind of illusory freedom ... Christ [is] the one who brings man freedom based on truth ..." (*RH* 12).

Freedom is truly free only when the person chooses the true good. Persons bound by addiction cannot remain in that bondage and fully become the persons God has created and called them to be. Addictive behaviors interfere with their relationships and work, and they experience tremendous pain. Instead of loving in an authentic manner, they regretfully isolate and numb themselves. They are led by painful decisions to avoid real love and experience frequent disconnection from the authentic happiness of life. They often are aware of the pain and the power of the addiction but are driven to continue the harmful pattern.

We can even become addicted to something that is supposed to be good for us. The thing to which a person is addicted is known as the *object of the addiction*. The object of the addiction can vary. A person's relationship with the object of the addiction is painful and causes damage to his or her life and to the lives of others. The pain of addiction permeates human life, personal health, marriage, and families. In addition, there are adverse effects on society, creativity, occupation, and resources.

2. How do we know if an addiction is present?

An addiction may be evident when a person maintains a relationship to such things in a manner that damages the person's life and/or the lives of others. In a strict sense, an addiction is most likely present when a person shows evidence of high tolerance to the object of the addiction as well as withdrawal. Basically, this high tolerance means that the addicted person needs more and more of the substance, chemical, activity, or sensation to which he or she is addicted in order to get the same level of effect, satisfaction, fleeting thrill, or exhilaration. The person is willing to take greater risks and invest a great deal of time to sustain that effect. A person may begin with regular or casual use and then accelerate to uncontrollable use. He or she may experiment with substances in the hope of attaining some kind of benefit, such as increased efficiency or relief from pain. A person begins by thinking he or she can control the substance, but the substance or activity ends up controlling him or her.

If the person is unable to access the object of their addiction or does not continue to interact with it, whether it be alcohol, narcotics, sexualizing, shopping, or work, physical and emotional symptoms of withdrawal may occur. These symptoms have a range of severity that include uneasiness, agitation, anxiety, inability to eat or sleep, sweating, racing heart, tremors, convulsions, threats to physical health, and even death.

3. You mentioned that a person can be addicted to a wide range of things, from chemical substances to sensations to activities. Are those things you mentioned all bad things to be avoided?

As we know from the Book of Genesis, all that God has created is "very good" (Gn 1:31). It is our poor choices in regard to the use of good things that cause pain and suffering. Sometimes this suffering takes the form of an addiction. Ordinarily, when suffering with an addiction, a person experiences some effect from the addictive substance or activity. The effect is usually a temporary-yet-intense feeling of satisfaction, exhilaration, or perhaps a numbing sensation. This effect is known commonly as a "high." The high temporarily and dramatically changes the person's mood. A person who is addicted begins to pursue the high to such a degree that other good things in his or her life are neglected and begin to suffer.

4. What are the specific dangers with a "high"?

The danger with the addiction in general and the high in particular is at least twofold.

First, the high is most often used to offset or block the feeling of some other pain in a person's life. This pain may be an emotional hurt that has accumulated over a number of years and has not yet healed.

Second, the person is willing to go to extraordinary lengths to ensure that the high continues as long as possible and occurs as often as possible. The object of the addiction, which provides the high, begins to become the most important thing in a person's life, more important than his or her well-being, family, education, occupation, children, physical health, and even his or her relationship with God. It is important that we address the pain in our lives in healthy ways and that we relate in a mature fashion to our responsibilities and relationships. Addiction hinders personal health in these important areas.

Drugs and those things to which we can become addicted never lead us to discover the meaning of life. They often lead us instead to numbness, passivity, violence, and alienation.

5. Can a person have more than one addiction?

Yes. If a person has more than one addiction, he or she is said to be struggling with "cross-addiction." For example, a person may be addicted to alcohol and also to Internet gambling. Or a person may be addicted to nicotine through smoking and also to alcohol. It is important to distinguish the addictions so that the person can receive proper care in ways that address each particular addiction.

Addictions are connected in other ways as well. For example, a person who is addicted to a drug such as cocaine may gamble online in hopes of securing enough money to purchase the drug. He may then steal money to feed both addictions. Addiction very rarely stays in one corner of our lives. It begins to spread out and affect everything.

6. What are the effects of addictions on young people?

One of the great blessings of young people is their originality, their spontaneity, and their curiosity. Sometimes a consumer culture and an ethos that values only pleasure can induce young people to experiment with very unhealthy and dangerous things. In addition to the conventional drugs, both legal and illegal, of which we ordinarily hear mention, the young are vulnerable to non-conventional addictions of which we might not be so aware. One of these is known as "huffing." This is a high that is obtained through the inhalation of solvents or various aerosol spray products.

Young people face a myriad of challenges and pressure in their lives. Today, many young people are affected by a troubled family life or a broken home. Many face daily pressures of a culture that equates worth with how much they acquire in material goods. When it is time for them to consider an occupation or plan a course of higher education, some are faced with excessive competition to fit in and to choose the field that will earn them the most money. They are pressured by commercial advertisements about the way they look, whether they are athletic enough or not, smart enough or not. Advancing from one's current social class and achieving a higher income bracket are the main messages behind much of the advertising we see. Television and fashion magazines portray alcohol as refined and sophisticated.

All of these pressures mount on the shoulders of our young people. Sometimes they are just looking for a way to escape the tension, to get away from all the noise, and to feel better. They may misuse prescription drugs belonging to themselves or to others, or turn to illegal drugs in an attempt to soothe themselves. Unfortunately, the many faces of addiction are all around us. We must offer to our young people healthy and holy ways of growing up, of finding their vocation, of coping with ordinary stress, and of reducing unhealthy stress. We must introduce them to a way of life that assists them in following the call to holiness.

7. You mentioned that even activities and events can be addictions. Can religion or even God be an addiction?

God himself, properly known and loved as he has revealed himself to mankind, can never be an addiction. God is love (1 Jn 4:8). We can approach God only through authentic love and the true gift of oneself to others, which is the very opposite of the kind of behaviors described above in connection with addiction. Worship and devotional practices are meant to communicate the mystery of the love of God and to draw us to his mystery through his glorification.

This having been said, a person may misappropriate some of the practices associated with religion in such a way — typically, a very self-centered way — that a person's performance of these rituals takes on the characteristics of an addiction. We refer to scrupulosity as an excessive preoccupation with unhealthy fear and guilt that prompts us to engage in religious practice in an unrealistic manner, as if it were one's own pious practices rather than the love of God that would bring about what is sought or desired. In such an unhappy situation, a person may unknowingly be living in an oppressive relationship — *not* with the God who graciously makes himself known through supernatural revelation and freely bestows his grace through the sacraments, but rather with a false and often harsh image of God stemming either from one's own poor understanding or from the misguided teaching or example of others.

Often the scrupulous person thinks continuously about sin to the point of despair, repeating religious practices compulsively in an attempt to offset an unhealthy fear and perceived guilt. This can be a difficulty for a great number of people. Persons who suffer with scrupulosity require kind but firm and insightful guidance. A good spiritual director and confessor can lead them to recognize God's love for them in such a way that gradually dispels the unhealthy guilt and fear from which they suffer.

8. Is addiction a sin?

The Church teaches that sin is an offense against God. Sins contradict right reason and can be categorized as mortal and venial (see *Catechism of the Catholic Church*, 1854-1863).

A *mortal sin* is an offense against God that involves serious or grave matter, has the full consent of the person's will, and is carried out with sufficient reflection from the person's intellect. By committing such sins, we say in effect that we do not want the life of God in our heart.

A *venial sin* is a deliberate offense against God in a lesser matter. Such sins diminish and wound the life of God in the soul.

Because addiction enacts such an undue influence on the person, the person's will often is impeded to some degree. Full consent of the will is required for a sin to be considered mortal. If full consent is not present, but the act involves serious matter, the sin remains a serious problem, but it is not mortal sin. In such a case, the personal fault of the individual may be diminished (*CCC* 1860).

Nevertheless, the individual's actions with regard to the addiction still harm one's human dignity and often harm the dignity of others as well. Even with diminished fault, the addicted person still retains a level of responsibility for his or her actions. He or she has an obligation to take all possible means to avoid the repetition of objectively immoral actions, especially with the help of a confessor, a spiritual director, and any other forms of assistance that may prove necessary, such as counseling or support groups of people in recovery from addiction. If it is necessary for one to seek professional psychological counseling or therapy, it will be important — especially in the case of some addictions involving issues of moral concern for Catholics — that the professional counselor or therapist should respect the moral values taught by the Church.

The Church exhorts each person to discern the level of seriousness of sin, including whether the sin is mortal or venial, with a wise confessor and/or prudent spiritual director. This includes circumstances in which an addiction may be present.

PART II:
THE IMPORTANCE OF A ROBUST CHRISTIAN ANTHROPOLOGY

9. Is addiction, then, a spiritual issue?

Addiction is a human issue that touches the person on many levels, including the spiritual level. We are created in the image and likeness of God (Gn 1:26-27) and are therefore created good (Gen 1:31). Anything that harms our dignity or the dignity of another person is a spiritual issue.

The study of the human person is known as anthropology. The subject of *anthropology* in the contemporary Western world is usually divided into several sciences such as sociology, history, linguistics, cultural studies, and archaeology. The European sense of the term, however, is grounded above all in the study of man in his very identity from a philosophical and theological point of view.

When we study the human person, we understand that man is created good. The human person is a union of body and soul. Man has an inherent tendency to pursue and choose to unite himself with that which is good, true, and beautiful. We also must be discerning, however, in those pursuits. We know that although man is inclined toward the good, he is sometimes attracted toward *apparent goods* that are not truly good for him. Because of Original Sin (Rm 5:12; Gn 3: 1-20) and its effects, we are wounded as we seek to discern what is truly good. The body can wage war against the soul (cf., Rm 7:23). The inner identity of man can be drawn away from perceiving the true good. In particular, the appetites that are meant to lead us to the good can become distorted and prompt our reason and will to choose apparent goods. Not every feeling we may have leads to something truly good. Instead, sometimes our feelings may lead to something that only *appears* as good but is actually harmful to us.

The Desert Fathers were highly influential Christian monks of the fourth and fifth centuries. They are known for their acute awareness of the spiritual life. Even though they lived in the desert, many persons sought their counsel. Their instruction was not like ordinary advice. The words of the Desert Fathers were permeated with salient wisdom and were expressed in short "sayings" that clarified various truths of the daily life of the Christian.

The Desert Fathers wrote about temptation by saying that the human person is being presented with counterfeit goods. The currency at the time of the Fathers was coinage. The coins were made of precious metal and struck with the authentic image of the monarch by a legitimate minter. Counterfeits could thus be recognized in one of three major ways: First, the image of the monarch was correct, but the metal was a mere painted, imitation gold; second, the counterfeiters made use of authentic gold, but the image was inauthentic and flawed; and third, the image was authentic, and the metal was authentic gold, but the minter was unauthorized. Each successive type of counterfeit was more difficult to detect than the one before it. Careful discernment was required to find the authentic currency and retain value for one's transaction. In the Christian life, the Fathers would say, we must be adept at discerning the counterfeit goods that the world places before us (John Cassian, *The Conferences* I. XX. 1; I. XX. 2; II. IX. 1). They may look legitimate, but upon closer examination we can detect the flaws of these counterfeit goods. We must take the time before making our choices to discern which is the authentic good. If we do not, we run the risk of being drawn in to what is less than real.

Most often, an addiction develops over a period of time. While the choices a person makes early on may influence the onset of the addiction, it may not be correct to designate an addiction simply as a character defect in the person. Addiction is not simply a matter of a person having a weak will. Rather, as an addiction advances in a person's life and behavior, the will becomes so clouded and the appetites so numbed that the addiction takes on the characteristics of a disease from which the person needs healing. Addictive acts do proceed from the person, but freedom often is impaired to a considerable extent by the addiction itself. Persons who are caught in compulsion are less able to see the full range of choices available to them.

In summary, addiction is not unrelated to human sin and sinfulness, but neither is it simply to be identified with sin. Once caught in the cycle of addiction that may indeed involve objectively sinful behavior, the person involved is unable to escape from the cycle of addictive behavior without the help of God and of other human beings. Even so, the person has the moral obligation to seek the assistance necessary to reform his or her life. Among the various forms of help that are needed are the spiritual assistance provided by the sacraments (especially the Sacrament of Penance), solid Christian teaching, good pastoral direction, supportive communities, and healthy religious practice.

10. Why do we want to choose things that only appear to be good or that may be harmful to us?

Since we are created good, we have an overall inclination to choose the good. We also have appetites. I am not referring simply to the craving we all feel right before lunch or dinner, but to appetites in the classical sense. Theology makes reference to various forms of human appetite, namely the *sensible, irascible,* and *concupiscible* appetites. Our appetites are good, but they need to be guided by reason. As I mentioned, due to the effects of sin, we find it difficult to recognize what is truly good.

Human persons experience a range of cravings within our senses. We can become hopeful or despairing, fearful or courageous or angry; we experience love and hate, desire and aversion, pleasure and sadness. Sometimes we can want something so much that we think we absolutely need it. When we feel we need it above all else, we might pursue it in a disordered way, or we might so overindulge in it that we greatly harm ourselves or others. These are the signs that our addiction has taken root, especially when we try to meet our own intangible personal needs through our appetites.

11. So, choosing something that is only apparently good can actually harm us?

Yes. If we choose an apparent good rather than a true good, we may aggravate the appetites. The appetite for the true good remains unsatisfied, with the result that if we remain in our error, we will continue to seek more and more of the apparent good because of the superficial and momentary gratification that it provides. The appetite starts to exert a great deal of influence in our life and can even start to override reason. We continue to confuse the satisfaction of our craving with what is truly good. Our world becomes reduced to the pursuit of what we think our appetites demand rather than what is truly good. This can then lodge deeply in aspects of our nature, especially the physical and psychological aspects.

We have to return to our inclination toward what is truly good. We have to entrust ourselves to what is reasonable in this battle between the appetites and our inclination to the good. Even in the midst of the battle, the human person always remains in the image of God and retains the dignity of one for whom Jesus died. The grace of God and the renewal of human reason is always offered to the person who is in pain and suffering from an addiction. God wants to be close to all who struggle. A person always retains some measure, no matter how small, of an inclination to choose the good, even if it is manifested only in the desire to *desire* to be well again. We are called to entrust ourselves to this freedom, however fleeting it may appear. The counterfeit freedoms of the world seek to lure us away from the freedom of the children of God. Pope John Paul II stated, "[M]an's true freedom is not found in everything that the various systems and individuals see and propagate as freedom..." (*RH* 12). Learning to be truly free takes a long time, and it must come from deep within the person.

This connection between freedom and truth is something upon which Pope John Paul II reflected many times during his pontificate, especially in his important 1993 encyclical *Veritatis Splendor* ("The Splendor of Truth"). When one understands well the connection between truth and freedom, it becomes clear that Catholic moral teaching — along with the Church's teaching about God, the Church, and the sacraments — do not in any way limit people's freedom. On the contrary, they help people to be freed from their own sinfulness and from the forces that arise through addiction as they come to know God as he really is and to relate to him as their true Liberator.

12. What causes an addiction?

The cause of addiction is a complex issue. Addiction arises from many intersecting factors. Some experts believe there may be causes in our genetic makeup, which obviously differs from one person to the next. Some experts focus more on the environment in which a person is raised at home or which he or she experiences in school. Most likely there is some interaction between our physical makeup and our environment.

A common factor in the presence of an addiction is pain. When we experience pain in our lives, particularly if this pain occurs early in life and is repeated over time, we tend to develop patterns of seeking comfort and relief from the distress. Even low levels of pain over time can affect us to the extent that we develop unhealthy ways of coping. Addictions can arise out of misguided attempts to heal pain from earlier in life.

Sometimes other people introduce a person to behaviors and model poor choices that make him or her more vulnerable to addiction. At some point along the way, the person also begins to make a choice or a series of choices that leads deeper into the addiction. We say this not to blame such individuals or make them feel guilty, but to help them realize that they can also make decisions that can help them heal. Perhaps surprisingly, to admit to having made wrong decisions can be quite a liberating discovery! Someone who looks only at what others have done to him or her will always feel like a victim, but someone who can say about any part of the experience that "I made the wrong decision" can now freely choose otherwise and may therefore stand, with God's help, at the beginning of a renewed life.

Even after a person has been in recovery from an addiction, he or she may fall back into the old patterns. A transition in life, the loss of a loved one, a change of job, school, or health can bring back old vulnerabilities. This is why ongoing support is so necessary for maintaining good health.

At times there may be underlying psychological issues that influence the addiction.

13. How does one know if one has an addiction?

As I mentioned, the classic signs are tolerance and withdrawal. There is a difference between having a problem with something, having a bad habit, and having an addiction. One should not immediately conclude that because one is having a problem with a craving or a bad habit that one has an addiction. The presence of an addiction is best determined in consultation with one's confessor or spiritual director, and a physician can provide the benefit of a thorough medical exam as needed. The wisdom of prudent guides often can help a person confront the denial and rationalization that can accompany an addiction.

There are self-tests that may be helpful for those of us who wonder whether we might have an addiction. Such resources from accredited health agencies can provide us with an initial insight into our behavior. They consist of a series of questions, the answers to which give some indication as to the nature of our behavior with regard to a specific substance or activity. These self-tests are often more reliable if we consult with our doctor about the responses.

14. **What are some practical signs through which one can tell the difference between a bad habit and an addiction?**

Just as we can become addicted to things, we can also form bad habits. Usually, the sequence of a bad habit can be broken with awareness of the habit and desire to change. An addiction is a bad habit that has become more resistant to change because of the development of other factors of dependency. An addiction differs from a bad habit in that with an addiction the person engages in the substance or the process more frequently and with more intensity. This leads to the development of tolerance and the presence of withdrawal symptoms that are hallmarks of addiction.

Through the honest admission that one has reached the limit of one's unaided powers, through a willing surrender to God's power to transform us, and then through an in-depth and honest examination of conscience, the reception of the sacraments, prayer, proper spiritual direction, and prudent use of wise professional guides, a person gains the insights and strength to allow new forms of behavior to displace the bad habit and thus to transform the addiction.

15. What is "the cycle of an addiction"?

The *cycle of an addiction*, or *addiction sequence*, is the phrase used to describe in general the series of experiences an addicted person undergoes within addiction.

Someone who is addicted tends gradually to reach a point of thinking continuously about the object of addiction. A man who is an alcoholic, for example, begins to obsess about the next drink. He is preoccupied with making sure he will be able to have alcohol and looks forward to it. Thoughts of drinking interrupt his day. If the drink is delayed, he becomes agitated and visibly uncomfortable. A woman who is addicted to shopping starts to arrange her schedule so that she can watch a "home shopping" show on television and purchase something or go out of her way to visit a mall.

The person next goes into a ritual phase. This signals that the onset of the addiction is getting closer. The alcoholic feels relief as he hears the ice cubes tumble into the glass at the bar. The person addicted to shopping feels more calm as she waits on the phone to give the credit card number after hearing that the item she wants to purchase is in stock.

Third is the behavior phase, in which the person acts out the addiction. The alcoholic drinks, the shopaholic buys, the addicted gambler places a bet. This can go on for hours.

Finally, in the fourth stage, the person acts on his addiction and feels guilt and despair. He has done it again. Amid this despair, he needs to feel comfort. The need for comfort to take away the despair gets him back to the first phase, thinking about the object of the addiction — the drink, the shopping, the bet. The cycle then becomes a self-perpetuating spiral of numbness falling downward with no foothold in sight.

16. This is a very serious situation, isn't it?

Yes. And what makes it much more serious and problematic is the way the Internet can intensify addiction. The Internet has entered our culture with amazing speed. The television of the 1960s was a huge box with a black-and-white screen with few channels and relatively high standards for the content that could be broadcast. By the mid-1990s, there was typically a personal computer in several rooms of a single house. A high-definition color screen allowed practically unrestricted access of highly immoral content into the most sacred spaces of our homes. The Internet has proven beneficial for various aspects of education and communication, but there has been a tremendous moral cost to the dignity of marriages, children, and families when the Internet has been used improperly.

The Internet has opened extremely detrimental venues at lightning speed into the American home and workplace. The temptation to abandon responsibility is stronger because many people presume they are anonymous as they browse through the vast world of cyberspace. Young people in particular are very vulnerable online. They never really know the true identity and motives of strangers whom they meet in chat rooms, virtual-reality games, and social-networking sites. In some cases, situations such as these become very dangerous.

PART III:
INITIAL APPRAISAL OF PROBLEMS
POSED BY THE INTERNET

17. How does the Internet pose problems to anyone susceptible to an addiction?

In 2002, the Pontifical Council for Social Communications released the document "Ethics in Internet." The document spoke about the value of the Internet but also the danger of exploitation, manipulation, and corruption in this particular medium. In fact, vices can be magnified through improper use of the Internet.

Prior to the availability of the Internet, if people wanted to gamble, they had to make an effort to seek out ways to gamble, such as travel to Atlantic City or Las Vegas; alternatively, they might seek out illegal means. Such effort provided a natural and important obstacle between people and the possible objects of addiction. These natural check-points of prudence allowed many people to think twice, to gather strength, resist, and forgo gambling — possibly because it was wrong for them, or because a complicated effort was required to gamble. The amount of effort involved in gambling would limit people's exposure to gambling, so it was somewhat easier to avoid.

The same may be said of pornography. Cultural disapproval of pornography, along with restrictions on its purchase, served as a natural boundary against easy access to pornography, whether in magazines or video. Natural boundaries and social taboos helped a person to avoid exposure to such activities.

Today, however, gambling is just a mouse click away, as are pornographic images, and both are available twenty-four hours a day. The glitter and lights of Las Vegas appear right on a person's computer screen through online gambling Web sites in the privacy of the home at any time of the day or night. Along with the lights, colors and the lure of winning, the person may experience an almost irresistible "rush." It is possible to place bet after bet, siphoning off one's hard-earned paycheck, diverting funds that would otherwise have been available for tuition, student loans, food, and savings. College students can sit in their dorm rooms and gamble using their bank accounts and credit-card accounts until they become fixated on winning. Instead, falling prey to the very laws of chance that makes gambling so profitable for those in the business, they eventually lose money more often than they win. They also lose time and, in some cases, their education and good name.

Many develop an obsession with the easy access of online gambling. They don't feel so alarmed when they see the decrease of digital numbers. An online debit transaction does not immediately register as a debit in a person's mind. It is not as vivid and immediate a sign of loss as would be the cash leaving one's pocket. Digital numbers seem different from paper money. The illusion is that the decrease of digital numbers in one's bank account is not as drastic as losing real cash. But it does add up, and it is very real. When the funds dry up, some will even turn to crime to get more money in the hope that the next bet will be the windfall.

18. The Internet really seems to complicate an addiction. What are the other areas of Internet addiction?

Pornography is a particularly significant online danger. There are over three billion Web pages online that convey sexually explicit images. A person can enter any number of pornographic websites and browse image after image without ever leaving home. This is one of the most seductive yet underreported dangers of contemporary society. Internet pornography is already a leading cause of the failure of marriages.

Internet sexual addiction, or "cybersex," can affect persons who ordinarily would never have become involved with pornography. The supposed privacy, low financial expense, and easy access of the Internet induce people to take risks they would never have considered otherwise. A person can become deeply captivated by what appears to be an endless supply of virtual sexual images online that lure him into a fantasy world. He believes that no one else can know about his activity and that he is in a totally private world. But this supposed anonymity is an illusion, since information that may reveal personal data about the supposedly anonymous user can be transferred to others, even without one's knowledge. Besides pornographic images, people may become involved in "chat rooms" and develop seriously harmful relationships based entirely upon fantasy. They may access streaming video in which human beings — sometimes including needy adults or defenseless children – have been rendered pure objects of sexual gratification for others. Besides these examples, there are many other forms of electronically accessible material with pornographic content.

While it may begin with an apparently harmless attempt to take refuge in instantaneous and undemanding sexual gratification to deal with daily stress, the use of pornography is already disordered in its divergence both from God's plan for human sexuality and in its detrimental impact on the human psyche. In particular, it harms the person's capacity to enter into healthy, wholesome, and intimate personal relationships and creates a disconnection from real life.

Even so, the pattern of addiction — and the development of a "tolerance" comparable to the diminishing effect of a certain quantity of alcohol — will frequently lead a person to seek pornographic content that is progressively more disordered. Having escaped into a totally private world where healthy social norms have been drowned out by the lure of instant sexual gratification, the person may easily fall into increasingly more reckless behavior. The danger to the person's overall well-being — and also to his family life and reputation — thus continues to rise as the behavior spirals out of control. This is a real danger for anyone who begins to develop such a habit, but it is especially a danger for men, given the proclivity of the masculine gender to the visual stimulation of sexual desire.

As this gets worse, a person begins to lie, act out, and go deeply into the addictive cycle. The addict becomes disconnected from real life and in some cases may begin to live a double life, acting out in secret in a manner that is contradicted by one's real-life status and daily activity. While pornography reduces persons to objects in servitude to a multi-billion-dollar industry, the person who is addicted to pornography either fails to see that he is participating in such exploitation of others or simply refuses to acknowledge the fact while indulging uncontrollably in the addictive habit. It is easy to see why the healthy intimacy of marriage suffers a great deal when one of the spouses becomes involved in such activities.

One must take decisive steps to decrease one's online vulnerability. If Internet access is necessary in the home, it might be best to keep the computer in a public area of the house where the screen is in full view of the door to the room. Software filters can be placed on the computer to help prevent the access to inappropriate content. Parents should closely monitor their children's online activities. In the absence of conflicting concerns of confidentiality, it might be helpful if the screens on one's work computer always face the door of the office or workspace. Adults can find a person with whom they can be forthright and honest who will monitor their online activities and provide accountability and support. Some forms of screening software or online services facilitate the sending of confidential usage reports to such a friend, the entrusting of filtering specifications to another person, the establishment of a locked account that can only be managed by means of a phone call to a professional technician, or other means of enlisting trusted partners who can support a person as he or she attempts to regain and preserve chastity in this struggle and break addictive patterns of behavior. In this, as in all struggles with addiction, a person especially must avail himself or herself to the life of grace and virtue made available in the sacraments.

PART IV:
THE SACRAMENTS:
THE IMPORTANCE OF GRACE AND VIRTUE

19. How does the Church advise one to care for an addiction, to return to the pursuit of true goods?

The teaching of the Church encourages all who struggle in any way, which includes those who suffer with addiction, to look upon Jesus (Jn 19:34). In him rests all our hope. When they look upon Jesus, those who struggle with addiction find the forgiveness of their sins and healing for their souls, and they are strengthened to foster the virtue of temperance, a good habit, in their life (CCC, 1809, 2341, 2730). The reception of the sacraments and the life of prayer lead both to our growth in virtue in general and to that of temperance in particular.

The Church also is aware of divinely ordained natural ways God can interact with us. For example, God makes known His love to us through the communio, that is, through the help and the communion with others that we find day to day in the Church, which signifies and makes present on earth the communion of the divine Persons of the Holy Trinity. Pope John Paul II, in his encyclical letter Evangelium Vitae ("The Gospel of Life"), referred to communities for treating addiction that have originated within the Church's mission of charity as "eloquent expressions of what charity is able to devise in order to give everyone new reasons for hope and practical possibilities for life" (EV 88).

Within such communities, an important form of assistance is found in intercessory prayer that always respects the privacy of persons, positive friendships, support groups, and the community of the Twelve Steps, all of which can compose a network of support for the person who is struggling with addiction. Also of great benefit is the assistance of persons in recovery who have struggled with addiction themselves. Many who have followed the path to recovery now help others along the same road. Such concentrated efforts of health care sometimes are absolutely needed for recovery. An addiction may claim so much of our lives that residential treatment in a therapeutic environment becomes advisable and necessary. Also important are programs that assist recovery and help the persons to develop new strategies as they re-enter day-to-day life. We must use all the good means God has given us to seek both health and holiness. All of these measures support the person burdened with addiction as he or she, with God's help, gradually moves from the slavery of addiction to the true freedom of a son or daughter of God. This is accomplished through the restoration of the person's free choice to embrace the principles and values of sobriety.

20. You mentioned virtue. What is virtue?

Virtue, as the Catechism of the Catholic Church states, is "a habitual and firm disposition to do the good. It allows the person not only to perform good acts, but to give the best of himself" (CCC 1803). It is clear, then, both that addictions hinder us in the pursuit of virtue and that the pursuit of virtue, especially with the strengthening that God provides through the grace of the sacraments, is both necessary and helpful in order to replace bad habits, including those connected with addiction. The Second Vatican Council affirmed, "The purpose of the sacraments is to sanctify men, to build up the body of Christ, and, finally, to give worship to God" (SC 59). We are very familiar with the teaching that sacraments cause grace, a sharing in the life of God, in our lives. However, according to St. Thomas Aquinas, sacraments also cause and nourish virtue in us. Virtue is a good quality of mind by which we act rightly. Virtue is a habit, but not in the sense of an action we repeat so often that we do it without thinking.

In the pursuit of virtue, it is important to avoid a kind of erroneous thinking that would be harmful and painful for anyone but especially one who struggles with addiction — namely, that "living a good life is simply up to me. I have to keep trying repeatedly until I get it right. I am left to my own devices." The line of thought proceeds like this: "All I have to do is to try harder to be good. If I am not good, then I am simply not trying hard enough." This is not the proper understanding of virtue in the tradition.

St. Thomas Aquinas speaks of virtue as a habit in the sense of the Latin word habitus, a dwelling or a disposition within us that strengthens us to chose to do the good (STh. Ia IIae q. 71, a. 1), and as "a good quality of the mind, by which we live righteously, of which no one can make bad use, which God works in us without us" (STh. Ia IIae q. 55, a. 4). St. Thomas' emphasis on the notion that God works the virtues "in us without us" is crucial. We open our hearts in docility to God, and he provides strength and guidance so that our choices and actions are transformed through the influence of His love, and we thus begin to act in a way that is in accordance with His Word.

21. What is the virtue of temperance?

The virtue of temperance is the strength God places in us to grow in holiness in regard to our appetites. The Catechism of the Catholic Church calls it "the moral virtue that moderates the attraction of pleasures and provides balance in the use of created goods" (CCC 1809). All believers must be docile to the summons of the Holy Spirit to temperance. Those who struggle with addiction can benefit greatly from making use of the strength afforded through this virtue.

St. Augustine and St. Thomas Aquinas, two great saints and Doctors of the Church, instruct us on the importance of temperance. Temperance is built up in us through grace. When we receive the sacraments, the Holy Spirit is at work within us with his seven gifts. The seven gifts of the Holy Spirit are wisdom, understanding, counsel, courage, knowledge, piety, and fear of the Lord (Is 11:2). According to St. Thomas Aquinas and Pope John Paul II, the gifts of fear of the Lord and piety help the virtue of temperance to grow within us (STh. Ia IIae, q. 68, a.4; John Paul II, Man and Woman He Created Them: A Theology of the Body [Boston: Pauline Books and Media, 2006] 353).

22. How do the gifts of fear of the Lord and piety assist the virtue of temperance?

The gift of fear of the Lord is not to be confused with anxiety or dread of God. Rather, through the gift of the fear of the Lord, the Holy Spirit begins to transform us. He makes our hearts more open to understanding and believing that God is our loving Father. We are drawn away from living a worldly way of life, which is so often bound up with fear. We fear we are not enough for the world, that we do not make enough money, are not good-looking enough, are not strong enough, not athletic enough, not smart enough, or not popular enough. It is on just such painful and negative images of ourselves that addictions thrive.

When we receive the sacraments, the grace of Christ enters into us and the Holy Spirit begins to soften our hearts to turn to God as our loving Father who forgives and accepts us. Our awareness and appreciation of our status as children of God is strengthened by the sacraments. We are no longer mesmerized by the fear of the world, for the love of God replaces that fear. Instead of preoccupation with self-doubt and perceived shortcomings, we are concerned with the mystery of God.

When we live as children of God, we are led to see others as children of God and the world as God's gift to us. The gift of piety strengthens us to act with the virtue of justice. We are strengthened to honor God and to respect our fellow human beings. We gain strength to treat others as our brothers and sisters and not use them as instruments of our addiction or neglect them because of our addiction. We also gain a just sense of stewardship for the world as God's gift. We are strengthened to refrain from using creation in an improper manner, as occurs frequently in the case of addictions.

When we are strengthened to see God as our Father — while also seeing one another as brothers and sisters and the world as God's gift — we know that temperance has taken root in our appetites and that our appetites have begun to be transformed by the grace of Jesus under the impetus of the Holy Spirit.

23. What about willpower? Can't the person just stop the addiction?

Two great dangers of an addiction are denial and overemphasis on willpower alone. Denial is common. A person who may be suffering from an addiction may often deny the situation to himself and others. It is important that we trust others who are knowledgeable and who care for us. Sometimes they can see destructive patterns in our behavior that we cannot or do not want to see.

The overemphasis on willpower is problematic because, in cases in which we do see a destructive pattern of addiction, we may try to stop it on our own, with only our strength of will. Often this does not work, and the person returns to the addiction. A pattern then develops: The person makes a resolution to stop the addictive behavior, setting off a chain of events. The person becomes stressed, begins to crave comfort, and finally returns to pursue the object of the addiction in order to feel better. Then follows a feeling of guilt along with a resolution to not do it again, and the whole cycle of addiction starts over. Ironically, this deliberate resolution, while in one sense reflective of the positive desire to change, nonetheless can actually be part of the addictive pattern. The resolution to stop often competes with the temptation of the addiction such that the resolution can soon fade. The person may act out again and then languish over a perceived failure. The addicted person is then caught in a cycle from which he is unable to free himself by his own unaided powers.

At one point, the person struggling with an addiction must make the decision to stop using the object of the addiction. He or she may fail many times thereafter. But this decision to begin a new way of life, and support this decision, is crucial. The decision to stop, however, must also be a decision to begin — to begin a new way of life, to entrust oneself to God, to change the daily self-defeating thought process which so often leads to the painful be-haviors of addiction. Through the grace-filled alteration of self-defeating thoughts, a person gains the strength to change one's lifestyle.

Recovery from addiction is about more than stopping a behavior; it is about beginning a new way of trust.

24. What are some practical ways to foster the virtue of temperance where addiction is present?

We receive grace and the strengthening of virtue through the sacraments. This strength is complemented through the help of one another in the communio of the Church. In particular, through the help of God's Word and of perceptive counselors, we learn to transform our old ways of thinking into new ways. As St. Paul said, "Our old self was crucified with Christ ... Now if we have died with Christ, we believe that we will also live with him" (Rm 6:6, 8).

St. Paul was not referring just to our physical death at the end of our lives. He was also referring to our death to self in all the ways in which we forgo our pride, our thinking that we know better, while we allow those who care for us to help us. This, in fact, is a form of asceticism — a term that refers to the spiritual practice of casting away from ourselves anything that prevents us from living the Gospel of Jesus. When we seek the strength to allow God to transform our old ways of thinking, we are practicing a form of interior asceticism.

One way we can do this is by challenging our "old ways" of thinking. Some people suffer for a long time with very negative ways of thinking, often believing that they are bad or far away from holiness. They magnify their mistakes and minimize their good points. It is important that such people begin to restructure their ways of thinking into truer and more positive understandings. A helpful activity to remember is easily called to mind by the initialism HALT, which stands for "Hungry, Angry, Lonely, Tired." It helps us to recall that when we are feeling hungry or angry, we are more vulnerable to addiction. When we become needy through feeling lonely or tired, we are more likely to look for something to take these feelings away, to fix them. So often we choose things we think will comfort us when, in fact, these things only make the matter worse. If a businessman knows that going away on a business trip is a time of loneliness and temptation for him to engage in sinful or addictive behavior, for example, he must fortify himself by being docile to the work of grace and the strength of virtue, perhaps avoiding things that may in the past have led to temptation.

If we know when we are feeling hungry, angry, lonely, or tired, we are more likely to choose holy ways to handle these situations. This is one of the reasons why self-knowledge and the examination of conscience are important. St. Teresa of Avila repeatedly emphasizes the importance of self-knowledge in her autobiography and spiritual writings. She writes, "This path of self-knowledge must never be abandoned, nor is there on this journey a soul so much a giant that it has no need to return often to the stage of an infant..." (The Book of Her Life, 13.15). Elsewhere, she says, "...let your prayer always begin and end with self-knowledge..." (The Way of Perfection, 39.5). Such self-knowledge is really a form of humility (The Interior Castle, I. 2. 8).

St. Teresa's words about humility are vital for receiving the mercy of God. Humility is born of a true vision of the self before God. Self-knowledge is the continual calling to mind of the fact that we are mere creatures, and that God is our Father and Creator. He created us on the basis of what is highest, the breath of God, and what is lowest, the clay of the earth (Gen 2:7). As creatures of God, we depend on his constant address to us to sustain us.

Self-knowledge reminds us that we rely on God at every moment, especially when we are tempted to turn away, to turn to what is lower than us, to turn back to the old ways. God is always present and loves us very much. He is willing to give us his grace. Even when we fall repeatedly, God is ready to forgive us, heal us, and strengthen us. Humility is strengthened by honesty, openness, and a willing spirit. St. Ignatius of Loyola encourages the daily examen, or examination of conscience, in light of this self-knowledge and the mercy of God.

Someone who is thinking many negative thoughts easily begins to feel negative, thus becoming more susceptible to destructive behavior and to being more easily caught in the addictive cycle. Temperance begins with our docility to God and his ways, which makes us more nimble at exchanging the old negative thoughts for new, positive, and true thoughts — that we are loved by God, are lovable to others, and have a firm place in the world despite how we may have been hurt.

Additionally, through faithfulness to the work of grace in us, we begin to contemplate God's love in simple ways. We slow down inner processes and begin to heal inner pain and hurtful memories. Through all of this, we develop and rely on a network of support and cut down on the chaos in our lives. A crucial aspect of any support system is that we have to have someone to whom we tell the truth. We can't keep secrets about these painful things. We must first of all tell God and also a trusted spiritual director or adviser. Then, our thinking is more true; our feelings begin to be more positive, and our actions are more likely to be good and holy.

25. How can the sacraments help us in the struggle with an addiction?

The sacraments make the love of Jesus effective within us. Jesus is the one who has suffered the most. He knows every suffering. On the Cross, he was deserted by all the apostles but one. He was rejected by the people. He was beaten and spat upon by the guards. He knows all of our pain. Jesus is there to help everyone, especially those who feel abandoned, overwhelmed, rejected, or who struggle as if they do not fit in, or who may feel themselves to be "losers." Jesus died on the cross to reveal the Father's love for us and to save us from sin. He sends the Holy Spirit to show us his love. Through the sacraments, the Holy Spirit brings the love and strength of Jesus into our hearts. Only his love can transform us permanently. His love is made available to us in many forms, but the first form is found in the sacraments.

Routinely in catechesis we place treatment of Baptism, Confirmation, and Holy Eucharist together. In the present context, it may be better to treat Baptism and Confirmation first, then to explain Penance, followed by the Holy Eucharist.

26. How do the Sacraments of Baptism and Confirmation help one who struggles with an addiction?

Jesus instituted the Sacrament of Baptism to communicate the life of grace so that man might be conformed to the image of Jesus in his Passion, Death, and Resurrection. Through this union with Christ in Baptism, Original Sin and any personal sin committed is forgiven. The baptized becomes an adopted son or daughter of God and is incorporated into the body of the Church. Each of these effects is important for those who struggle with addiction. God has sealed the baptized with an indelible mark that they belong to Christ and can call on him with strength of that union as a son or daughter.

God is very familiar with the pain of those who suffer. The history of the world is the history of salvation. God has acted in many wondrous ways to rescue and deliver man from bondage and slavery. At the foundation of the world, the Spirit hovered over the waters (Gen 1:2) to create the world and then to create man from nothing. Creation itself is a salvific delivery from nothingness. God delivered his people from bondage throughout the Old Testament, including at the Deluge (Gen 8-9; Pet 3:20), and at the Red Sea (Ex 13: 17 ff.).

God is always faithful to his love. He hears those who call on him and supplies his grace for their transformation. This includes in particular those who need deliverance from addiction. Baptism initiates us into the life of Christ and draws us close to him. Those who suffer with addiction can be assured that in Baptism they have been joined to Christ in a way that gives them strength to journey toward healing. God can repeat in the midst of the cycle of addiction the effect of the saving action by which they were sealed in Baptism: the victory of Jesus on the Cross.

The Sacrament of Confirmation is necessary for the completion of baptismal grace (*CCC* 1285). Through the anointing with oil and the laying on of hands, the person receives the fullness of the outpouring of the Holy Spirit begun in Baptism. The confirmed are rooted more deeply into the Sonship of Jesus; as they are more firmly united to Christ, the gifts of the Holy Spirit are poured forth in them in abundance. Through this outpouring, the confirmed person is more perfectly bound to the family of the Church and receives the special strength of the Holy Spirit to spread and defend the faith (*CCC* 1302).

The special strength received from the Holy Spirit in Confirmation penetrates deeply into the soul of the person. The sacrament leaves an indelible mark on the soul and the person can call on the special assistance of the gifts of the Holy Spirit. As was already mentioned, the gifts are vital to the daily living of the Christian life, especially for those who struggle with addiction. In particular, the gifts of fear of the Lord and of piety, both understood in their proper sense, are crucial to those who journey through recovery from addiction. These gifts help undermine the causes of addiction and allow the person to begin the journey to freedom in the grace of God.

27. How do the Sacraments of Penance and the Holy Eucharist help someone who is struggling with addiction?

The Sacrament of Penance is the ordinary means by which God forgives sins. Everyone needs to celebrate this sacrament whenever he or she is aware of having committed grave sin. The Church also recommends frequent confession of any venial sins one has committed.

When one is struggling with addiction, it is sometimes difficult to know whether one has committed mortal sins or not because the will has been so compromised by addiction. Sometimes one is conscious of actions that are gravely wrong, but unsure of how much freedom was involved. The important thing, however, is that whatever the degree of actual guilt that may be involved, this sacrament — when celebrated as honestly as possible and with good faith — always brings us the mercy of Jesus. His mercy alone heals us from any wrongs we have done to ourselves or to others. Through the gift of his mercy, we are able to hear, internalize, and realize that we have been forgiven.

Freed from our sins, we can devote ourselves all the more to the journey of healing begun in the Sacrament of Penance.

The sacraments are not magic; rather, they are a personal encounter with the Lord who has real power to heal us. They admit us to the redemptive grace of Jesus and make the mysteries of Christ effective in our lives. Through the acts of the penitent, the one confessing opens his or her heart to God.

According to the Church's teaching, there are four essential parts to the celebration of the Sacrament of Penance — contrition, confession, priestly absolution, and satisfaction.

1. The *contrition* of the penitent involves sorrow of heart for having wandered from the path of Christ and confidence in the power of God to restore the penitent to the path of uprightness and healing.

2. The *confession* of sins expresses not only the sins we have committed, but also it expresses at the same time our trust that God is faithful to his love. He promises to receive, forgive, and heal us.

3. The *absolution* imparted by the bishop or priest constitutes the moment of forgiveness, healing, and restoration to the fold of Christ. These realities of forgiveness and mercy are important to every person, and they may

be so in a particularly powerful way for those who suffer the pain of addiction.

4. The *satisfaction* — that is, the performance of penance — is the sign that the penitent performs to render humble gratitude to God for his patient love and to begin to live the Christian life under the renewed impetus of grace.

The Holy Eucharist is the sacrament of the Lord's Body and Blood. At the celebration of Mass, the bread and the wine are transformed to become the sacramental real presence of the Body and Blood of Jesus. This is how Jesus shows his love for us. He gives us himself to nourish us through unity with him. The healing that was begun in the Sacrament of Penance is now deepened by the nourishment received in the Eucharist. Whenever we may have committed grave sins, it is through the Sacrament of Penance that we prepare ourselves to approach once more this banquet of the Lord's Body and Blood.

Besides the actual reception of the Lord's Body and Blood in Holy Communion, adoration of the Holy Eucharist that is reserved after Mass in the tabernacle in Catholic churches provides us time to be alone with Jesus and pray to him. Such time spent in adoration before the Lord's Real Presence in the Blessed Sacrament is particularly helpful to persons struggling with addiction and in recovery from addiction because it places one in conscious proximity to Jesus. He alone knows the secret places of our heart and still has today the same power that we see him exercising in the Gospels, that of healing our souls, minds, and bodies. Adoration before the Blessed Sacrament, for whatever length of time we can spend there, provides refreshment and peace for us in the presence of God's unique love.

PART V:
THE IMPORTANCE OF PRAYER

28. Does the Church have any particular prayers that help us to grow in temperance?

Yes. In addition to the sacraments, pondering and praying over all of the mysteries of the life of Jesus is also a great help to the life of grace. In particular, praying the Rosary is an excellent way to meditate on the life of Jesus. As Pope John Paul II said, the Rosary is "the school of Mary." The Blessed Mother, in her union with the Lord, is the model of temperance for us. When we contemplate the mysteries of the life of Jesus with the Blessed Mother, she teaches us how to "treasure these things" — the mysteries of Jesus — in our hearts (Lk 2:19). This silent, meditative "treasuring" teaches us to slow the momentum of our hearts and minds for Jesus. This momentum quells the uproar of worldly fear that so often and so easily stirs our appetites and leads into a storm.

There is also the Serenity Prayer, which will be familiar to many who have sought out the powerful support of groups following the Twelve Steps, which were developed first among recovering alcoholics and later used by those seeking to overcome a wide variety of addictions. This prayer sums up the style of trusting thought that is so crucial for someone who is trying to adopt a new way of thinking. In the Serenity Prayer, we pray:

"God grant me the serenity to accept the things I cannot change; the courage to change the things I can; and the wisdom to know the difference. Amen."

29. How does the Serenity Prayer help those who struggle with addictions?

The Serenity Prayer is a short prayer by which we ask God to transform our ways of thinking and our attitudes. We ask God to give us the grace to *accept what we cannot change*. So much of addiction is fueled by our ways of thinking, our refusal to accept reality. We would rather escape. We refuse to accept that we do not have as much money, perhaps as much talent, or the same type of parents or children as someone else. We think all our problems are someone else's responsibility, so that if *they* would only change, our own lives would be wonderful. Often we get so caught up with what we *do not* have in life that we forget what we *do* have. At the same time, we are tempted to think that everyone else is better off than we are. We may think we are mistakes. This negative thinking sets us up to want to escape life through becoming attached to something we think we can control that will make us feel better. Such a desire for escape can be a dangerous trigger for an addiction.

The Serenity Prayer reminds us to accept what we cannot change, to have courage to accept responsibility for our own lives and to change the things that we can, and to choose wisely in discerning between the two fields. The Serenity Prayer reminds us that while we may make mistakes, we never *are* a mistake.

The acceptance of the Serenity Prayer is not a *laissez-faire* attitude of resignation. Instead, it is a more-or-less steady abandonment to divine providence. This is the great theme of Jean-Pierre de Caussade, the eighteenth-century French Jesuit spiritual director and author. He saw that the key to all spiritual growth was to deliver oneself confidently into the hands of God. His book, *Abandonment to Divine Providence*, along with his letters, emphasizes this theme. In the face of our fears, doubts, and hesitations, we turn to rely on God's grace to awaken us to be attentive to him in a simple and ordinary manner.

PART VI:
THE TWELVE STEPS

30. Earlier, you mentioned the Twelve Steps. What are the Twelve Steps, and how do they relate to addictions?

The Twelve Steps are a series of realizations and actions that can help lead a person into a new lifestyle of recovery from an addiction. The Steps have been very helpful for many and are usually a part of a program of treatment for an addiction. They are also often part of maintaining recovery from addiction. In fact, the sequence of the Twelve Steps was developed in America. The Steps are best carried out with the assistance of a sponsor and in the midst of a confidential community that provides the opportunity for regular support meetings.

Various traditions of spiritual practice arise in the Church from time to time and come from various parts of the world. Some of these are associated with various "schools of the spiritual life." For example, the life and writings of St. Teresa of Avila and St. John of the Cross, the Spanish mystics, have enriched the school of Carmelite spirituality in the Church. St. Benedict founded his rule in Italy, and we refer to the Benedictine school of spirituality. From Germany there are the Rhineland mystics, and from France there is the Marian devotion of St. Louis de Montfort. Various parts of the world have made significant contributions to the spiritual life. From America, the system of Catholic education is a major contribution as particularly manifest in the work of St. John Neumann and St. Katharine Drexel. Some people also refer to the delineation of the Twelve Steps of Alcoholics Anonymous as a contribution of America to the spiritual life. The Twelve Steps, in one sense, are more a spirituality than a "treatment," which they embody to take "one day at a time."

The Twelve Steps are:

Step 1: We admitted we were powerless over our addiction — that our lives had become unmanageable.

Step 2: We came to believe that a Power greater than ourselves could restore us to sanity.

Step 3: We made a decision to turn our will and our lives over to the care of God as we understood him.

Step 4: We made a searching and fearless moral inventory of ourselves.

Step 5: We admitted to God, to ourselves, and to another human being the exact nature of our wrongs.

Step 6: We were entirely ready to have God remove all these defects of character.

Step 7: We humbly asked God to remove our shortcomings.

Step 8: We made a list of all persons we had harmed and became willing to make amends to them all.

Step 9: We made direct amends to such people wherever possible, except when to do so would injure them or others.

Step 10: We continued to take personal inventory and, when we were wrong, promptly admitted it.

Step 11: We sought through prayer and meditation to improve our conscious contact with God as we understood him, praying only for knowledge of his will for us and the power to carry that out.

Step 12: Having had a spiritual awakening as the result of these steps, we tried to carry this message to other addicts and to practice these principles in all our affairs.

As mentioned before, these Twelve Steps have been so effective in sustaining recovery from alcoholism that other programs of addiction treatment and recovery now employ the same Steps. For example, recovery from addiction to narcotics, sex, and food adapt the essence of the Twelve Steps for persons struggling in those areas.

31. **It seems as if some of the Steps are very conducive to the regular practices of the Catholic Faith. Is that true?**

Yes. One may say that virtually all of these Steps, taken individually, have been found in the spiritual heritage of the Church for centuries.

For example, the powerlessness of the first step is very consistent with the Church's doctrine of Original Sin. The act of entrusting expressed by Steps 2 and 3 is very much in harmony with the Catholic doctrine of justification, which we believe no one can earn by himself since it can only come about by God's power; it is also consistent with the virtue of humility and the words of Jesus to St. Paul: "My grace is sufficient for you, for my power is made perfect in weakness" (2 Cor 12:9).

The Fourth Step of the moral inventory is somewhat similar to the regular examination of conscience, while Step 5 evokes the confession of sins as an essential part of the spiritual life of all Catholics. Steps 6 and 7 are reminiscent of the Catholic doctrine concerning "actual grace" — that is, the supernatural help for a given moment that God gives to those who seek him in their struggles against evil. In a given instance, Steps 8 and 9 could very well be the same satisfaction or penance that a confessor might ask someone to perform after a good confession.

Steps 10 and 11 remind us of something the saints have always realized — namely, that conversion of heart is not something that happens in a single moment but continues throughout life. The emphasis on prayer in Step 11 is very similar to the injunction of St. Paul to "pray without ceasing" (1 Thes 5:17). Finally, Step 12 enjoins the very same kind of gratitude for God's grace that has led missionaries to every corner of the globe in order to share with others the saving message that they themselves had received.

The Twelve Steps can be of great benefit, especially in consultation with a confessor or spiritual director.

32. Can one outgrow an addiction with time?

Ordinarily, once a person has an addiction, they always "have" it. The healing occurs when the person who has an addiction lives in recovery, or sobriety, a time when the addictive behaviors are not present. Chronological aging does not in itself lead a person out of an addiction. Rather, one must internalize grace, virtue, growth, and maturity. Hopefully, we all advance in these qualities as we age, but aging itself does not ensure that we will grow in maturity. In fact, a secularized culture often reinforces attitudes that work against the internalization of virtue.

33. Is there a cure for addiction?

Many who have been addicted and those who have experience working with addiction tell us that there is no "cure" for addiction. Instead, there is recovery. One who has suffered with an addiction must remain vigilant that the addiction does not again overtake the healthier ways of acting that one has developed in recovery. As the Catechism teaches, "Self-mastery is a long and exacting work. One can never consider it acquired once and for all. It presupposes renewed effort at all stages of life" (CCC 2342).

Recovering addicts must retain a program of life, built upon many of the steps mentioned above, so that they remain healthy and free of addictive behavior. The road to recovery is not an easy one. Setbacks and "failures" are common when we attempt to change our lives and continue on the road to recovery. Struggling with an addiction should not be regarded as a stigma. It is a summons to care.

Addiction always causes great disturbance in marriages and families. It impacts the health of men and women and the well-being of children. One who notices the onset of addiction must never fall prey to the illusion that he or she will be able to control the behavior and forestall the serious consequences. Rather than waiting until he or she reaches the point of helplessness and "hits bottom," a person can perhaps learn from the stories of others what a dangerous road he or she has already begun to follow, one which will reach the same unpleasant destination if the addiction is not managed early on.

After a setback, we must get up again, seek forgiveness, forgive ourselves, and continue on the way to healing. To find the good news of the "culture of life" that is the Gospel, we have to empty ourselves of the bad news of the "culture of death" — the dead-end road that begins with promises of escape and immediate gratification but always ends in destruction.

The attitudes, beliefs, and practices that hide and even deny the dignity of the human person accumulate around us. Meanwhile, the Church must respond with the message that the human person, created in the image of God, is born for a greater destiny than that which is promised by the passing things of this world. Accordingly, the Church is able to help people to endure the suffering that they will experience when they let go of their addiction, and to show them the life of freedom that awaits them — even in this life — beyond the trials of the present moment.

The Church is always ready to listen to those who are suffering with addiction. They have to tell their story and express their pain, which helps them to yield to grace. Recall the woman presented in the fifth chapter of the Gospel of St. Mark. This woman had been in pain for twelve years. She had "suffered a great deal under the care of many doctors" (Mk 5:26). She only grew worse in her affliction. Then, she was prompted in faith to touch the hem of the garment of Jesus, which she thought would heal her (Mk 5:27-28). As soon as she did so, she was healed. Jesus realized that the power of healing had gone forth from him. He turned and asked, "Who touched me?" (Mk 5: 31). The woman came forward "and fell at his feet and, trembling with fear, told him the whole truth" (Mk 5:33).

We, too, must approach Jesus. Even if we are afraid, it is then that we must approach Jesus with all the more decisiveness. We, like the woman, must tell him the "whole truth" — the whole truth of how the world has pained us, of how we have hurt others and ourselves. We must show him our scars as he heals us with his wounds.

The Church, as she listens to the story of people's sufferings, stands ready, like the Good Samaritan (Lk 10:25-37), to pour the wine and oil of the sacraments into their wounds — not the addictive wine of the world, but the new wine that makes us strong and sets us free. No one, regardless of whatever wrong he or she may have committed, is outside the loving concern of the Church. No matter what other superficial attractions allure us, no matter how many times we may have fallen, the human spirit remains always attracted to freedom, and our Lord has entrusted to the Church the message of the truth that sets us free (Jn 8:32). This is not the false freedom of worldly autonomy, but the true freedom of the plan of God.

34. What measures can help prevent addiction?

The formation of a culture of life through the cultivation of a civilization of love is the overall measure which helps prevent addiction. A culture of life is also the best measure to address addiction adequately when it does take place.

The formation of such a culture includes a strong family life marked by love, respect, patience, and the practice of the faith. The family is meant to be the domestic Church, a place of charity and of the ability to speak to one another without fear, where father and mother are able to relate in love, and where children are permitted to grow and mature in holiness. Additionally, a regular involvement in the life of one's parish, in particular Sunday Mass and the celebration of the sacraments, can help to prevent addiction. The environment of Catholic schools and religious-education programs likewise contribute to the formation of a culture of life.

Awareness and education regarding the patterns and dangers of addiction, conveyed in appropriate and timely ways, can help prevent addiction. The news media and entertainment industry must promote appropriate forms of entertainment that advance the dignity of the human person, marriage, and the family. Civil government must promote and enforce guidelines to ensure that families and parents are provided adequate means to guide their children in accordance with sound development. In particular, children must have the means to know their infinite dignity and worth regardless of their social condition, and they must not be abandoned to the helplessness, loneliness, or boredom that would be likely to induce them to the adoption of addictive behaviors.

Society, too, must promote principles of prudence in manners of recreation, entertainment, and care for family life. An environment in which a person is accepted, supported, and encouraged to choose what is true and good is an atmosphere that helps to prevent addiction.

35. **Family members and friends of a person who has an addiction often suffer a great deal. Are there measures to assist them?**

Yes. So often the effects of addiction are not limited to the addicted person but spread outward and entangle those closest to them. The Church offers a great deal of pastoral support to those who are affected by having a loved one who struggles with addiction. The life of grace and virtue made available through prayer and the sacraments provides great strength for families and friends of persons who are caught in the cycle of addiction. There is also pastoral counseling, which is available by referral through local parishes and individual dioceses, in particular through the dedicated work of various agencies associated with Catholic Social Services.

Various organizations such as Al-Anon and Alateen have been established for family members and those who are close to persons with addictions. To some extent, the addicted persons, because of the nature of their suffering, often allow and enact a very difficult environment in which to live. Those close to them are greatly affected by this unpredictable and often unstable situation, which commonly involves repeated arguing, avoidance, denial, fear, conflict, unstable patterns of relation, and dashed hopes. Through such organizations as Al-Anon and Alateen, spouses, children, extended family, and friends of those who are addicted can find empathy, understanding, compassion, resources, and insight for developing healthy strategies of living.

CONCLUSION

Thank you for your time with us and the wisdom which you have shared.

Thank you very much. In the midst of the isolation of unrealistic expectations and the pain of addiction, we turn to "Christ Jesus our hope" (1 Tm 1:1), who took upon himself the suffering that is ours and bestowed on us the divine life that is his own. Only in his light can we find healing and strength.

I express deep admiration for all those who, through effective collaboration, help others carry the cross of addiction and help to instill in them the hope of renewed life. They have truly grasped the meaning of St. Paul's words: "Bear one another's burdens, and so you will fulfill the law of Christ" (Gal 6:2). I thank all who assist in the work of healing, in particular those who take part in the Church's mission as priests, deacons, religious men and women, and dedicated lay persons, who bear the delicate burden of calling the victims of addiction to accept responsibility for their lives even while helping them to know the infinite riches of God's mercy that is always available to them. I also express gratitude to those who work in the educational, research, medical, and clinical professional services, striving to help those who suffer with addictions. The contribution of each is appreciated and remains so necessary.

Finally, I offer my prayers for all those who are in recovery from addiction, for all those who struggle with an addiction, and all those who suffer in any way, especially those who have a family member or loved one afflicted with addiction. May the grace of Jesus Christ and the intercession of His Blessed Mother Mary guide them to healing and renew in them the freedom of the children of God.

March 2009

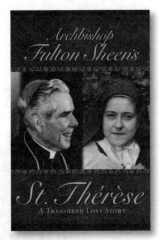

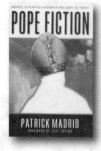